Stephen M. Jacoby

ARCHITECTURAL SCULPTURE IN NEW YORK CITY

With an introduction by Clay Lancaster

Dover Publications, Inc., New York

To Jordy Bell
For her encouragement, critical acumen
and shared sense of purpose

Published in Canada by General Publishing Company,
Ltd., 30 Lesmill Road, Don Mills, Toronto, Ontario.
Published in the United Kingdom by Constable and
Company, Ltd., 10 Orange Street, London WC 2.

Architectural Sculpture in New York City is a new work,
first published by Dover Publications, Inc., in 1975.

International Standard Book Number: 0-486-23120-8
Library of Congress Catalog Card Number: 74-15247

Manufactured in the United States of America
Dover Publications, Inc.
180 Varick Street
New York, N.Y. 10014

FOREWORD

In 1963, I came upon a chained-in, overgrown field where wild grasses hid salvaged debris of an earlier century, remnants from demolished brownstones. The carved faces looking blankly to the sky over the Brooklyn Museum intrigued me as sculpture, as symbols of the earlier city, and as patient subjects for the demanding eye of the camera.

The Brooklyn Museum now has the Frieda Schiff Warburg Memorial Sculpture Garden, where examples of various styles of building decoration survive, still on public view. But many figures and friezes have been broken in pieces and used as landfill for swamps and riverbanks. When I finally began this project in 1969, I was uncertain what I would find.

Walking throughout the city, examining its buildings in the way a tourist would look over the old quarter of a European city, I discovered that a fascinating variety still exists, albeit scattered and fragmentary, weathered and begrimed, and on the verge of extinction.

Few New Yorkers are aware of this heritage— one man who had walked the same street for thirty years first discovered the storybook illustrations on a building when my camera provoked his curiosity.

May this book do the same for others.

The photographs were taken with Nikon F and Nikkomat 35 mm. bodies and 50 mm. f/1.4 and 135 mm. f./2.8 Auto Nikkor lenses. While I had originally hoped to catalogue examples of sculptural embellishment on all architectural types extant in New York City, I soon discovered that some genres were far more engaging and retained more vitality than others under the technical limitations of 35 mm. black-and-white photography. The collection is also biased by personal taste for the animate, exotic and enigmatic.

Particulars have been supplied wherever information on the building was available.

STEPHEN M. JACOBY

Park Slope, Brooklyn
August 10, 1974

INTRODUCTION

The era covered in these photographs of sculpture visible from New York City's sidewalks begins at the time of the invention of the telephone and arc light, and goes up to the launching of the first moon rocket. This span, a few years short of a century, was inaugurated in the late 1870s, when the East Side elevated line was extended along Third Avenue as far north as 129th Street. In 1880, the West Side "L" commenced operation over a corresponding stretch of Ninth Avenue. Rail service, unimpeded by surface traffic, became available to both sides of Manhattan Island, flanking Central Park and upward, creating a building boom in these areas.

The row house of brownstone was just coming into full flower, following the building lull caused by the Civil War and its aftermath and the Depression of 1873. Brownstone itself, brought to New York from both east and west—notably from Portland in the Connecticut hills and the Belleville yards throughout upper New Jersey—had figured in the city's buildings since the Dutch settlement. Brownstone attained architectural status before the American Revolution, through its use in the portico, entablature, belt courses, quoins, door and window and other trim on Saint Paul's Chapel, dating from the mid 1760s, which had walls of native schist. Brownstone was employed for the high basement of New York City Hall, begun in 1803, the surface of which was replaced by red Minnesota granite revetments in 1954. The "mahogany" stone was popularized through selection for the walls of Richard Upjohn's Trinity Church, built on lower Broadway during 1840–1846. Constructed shortly afterwards was Minard Lafever's Church of the Holy Trinity (1844–1848), at Clinton and Montague Streets, Brooklyn, also of brownstone. Soon secular public buildings, such as Odd Fellows' Hall, at Grand and Centre Streets, Manhattan, and townhouses generally used the material on their facades. The Brownstone Age was launched.

Brownstone was not laid up as solid walls but was limited to street-front sheeting on otherwise brick and timber structures. The blocks were cut about four inches thick, the equivalent of one layer of brick. Because it could be worked easily when quarried, brownstone lent itself to an infinite variety of treatment, thereby permitting considerable decorativeness and individuality. By the middle of the nineteenth century, brownstone houses began to appear in Greenwich Village, the Gramercy Park and Murray Hill sections, and on Brooklyn Heights, as duplexes or as a few identical consecutive private dwellings on predominantly brick-facaded streets. By 1860 they spanned entire blocks up to 59th Street in Manhattan, and brownstones were spreading rapidly south and eastward in Brooklyn. During the last quarter of the nineteenth century, the brownstone became the characteristic New York City residence.

Many of the sculptures of the late 1800s in this book are of brownstone. However, others represent the change to other media already then in process. Brownstone is a sandstone. It is porous, layered and absorbs moisture. Water contracts with cooling until near the freezing point; then it expands more than it has contracted, becoming ice. The force of the expansion chips off the particles of sand composing brownstone, disintegrating it. Close-grained limestone (marble), hard granite, terracotta, iron and bronze are more durable, and came to be preferred over brownstone. Terracotta and the metals can be modeled in an easily worked material and baked or cast, thus eliminating the arduous chiseling process, the dust from which is injurious to the artisan's health. But the snob appeal of stone carving kept its production alive.

The city supported numerous yards cutting and selling stone. As most of the rock core of New York is the unattractive and poor-quality schist, facing stone had to be imported. The north tip of Manhattan and beyond is made up of marble, and ashlar was quarried and transported to the metropolis from nearby Westchester County. Most facing stone was brought from greater distances. The marble for the upper walls of New York City Hall came from Massachusetts. A good deal of limestone came from Bedford and other sites in Indiana. Yellow Berea sandstone came from Ohio. Granite came from New England, the distinctive pink variety from Quincy, Massachusetts. Terracotta and metal castings were supplied locally. The J. W. Fiske plant at 99 Chambers Street, Manhattan, and G. W. Stillwell Company at 38 Fulton Street, Brooklyn, were among the foremost producers of architectural ironwork. Besides terracotta, a practical substitute for stone was molded blocks of concrete, tinted to taste, such as the Beton Coignet used for the rich facade reliefs and in the vault of Cleft Ridge Span (1871–1872) in Prospect Park.

Authorship of early sculpture on buildings remains obscure. Architects planning buildings indicated spaces to be elaborated on elevation drawings, but reliefs were largely determined by the whims of anonymous carvers. Major architectural firms employed draftsmen who conceived the details on paper, yet their names are no more recorded than those of the masons. Undoubtedly established companies collaborated on successive undertakings, which fostered mutual understanding as to desired results between designers and executors. Most of the brownstone carvers were immigrants from the British Isles—English, Scottish and Irish—with some Germans and a few Italians. The Italians arrived as the demand for terracotta modeling increased. Slowly architectural sculpture was elevated to a fine art, and those who practiced it were given credit for their work alongside architects. In the following collection there are examples from the turn of the century by such well-known sculptors as John Quincy Adams Ward, Paul Bartlett and Daniel Chester French. More recent masters represented are Paul Manship, Leo Friedlander, Adolph A. Weinman, F. G. D. Roth and William Zorach.

City building facade features that were ornamented include arches, especially spandrels and keystone; applied orders, including the entablature (frieze and fascia), and the capital, shaft and base of piers and pilasters; door and window enframements, notably pediments over entrances, and apron plaques and cartouches under fenestration; corbels, caryatids and other supports for lintels or projecting cornices; openwork crestings, and parapet figures and finials; stairway railings and balcony addenda; and assorted panels and borders, and miscellaneous foci for relief of the architectural mass and delight of the eye. Subjects depicted consist primarily of the human form, masks, heads, busts, torsos and full figures; animals, both real and imaginary, lions, horses, birds, griffins and dragons; floral motifs, rinceau, leaves and blossoms, the classic acanthus and American sunflower; and a variety of abstract shapes, escutcheons, balusters, vases, crockets, trefoils and quatrefoils, consoles, modillions and dentils; and running moldings, notably the egg-and-dart and bead-and-reel designs.

The Reconstruction and modern periods in America sought inspiration from many sources, but it was not applied in such an imitative way as in the preceding era of the revivals. During late nineteenth-century eclecticism, motifs were not in themselves original, but designers at least exercised freedom in the way they put them together. The practice evolved to the creation of new forms. Inasmuch as city lot size and height restrictions on non-elevator buildings kept the dimensions and shapes of facades relatively constant, the remaining variable was ornamentation. As had been done before with stone, terracotta was shaped in the studio; but from this time onward unfinished stone blocks were set in place, and the carver exercised his imagination upon them *in situ*, as had ancient Aegean and medieval European carvers.

In this album of *Architectural Sculpture in New York City*, the camera has separated reliefs from their architectural context and presents them independently as a vital art form. Many types are represented, but the majority may be placed in seven or eight categories. Most show European influence. The exceptions are derived from the early civilizations of the Near East. Assyrian faces adorn the capitals of the old Temple of the Knights of Pythias on West 70th Street (No. 12), winged lion and bull reliefs enliven the frieze of the Fred F. French Building on Fifth Avenue (No. 106), and a dual-bodied feline caps the colonnette on the Transportation building at 225 Broadway (No. 105). Dating from the late 1920s, their stylization keyed in with the new abstracted forms of the Arts Décoratifs style.

It is surprising that the photographed examples show so little of the Greek and Roman manner, except through Renaissance and more recent European intermediaries. The Hellenes had no awareness of harmonizing sculpture with architecture, other than by fitting it into spaces reserved for it. Frieze reliefs and pediment sculptures in the round never expressed the structural or decorative character of the building, as did Gothic niche figures, projecting grotesques and gargoyles. Roman temple embellishments made no advance over their Greek predecessors. The group in the pediment of the Neo-Classic New York Stock Exchange (No. 117) displays the disregard of antique statues for environment, and here John Ward's anatomical naturalism is further alienated from architecture than had been the idealized Hellenic carvings. The slightly later figures in the tympanum of the Dime Savings Bank of Brooklyn (No. 137) are more successfully composed and better related in depth to the triangular enframement.

The next well-defined European style which lent itself to New York carvings is the Romanesque. It grew out of the Near Eastern Byzantine, an architecture that in its pure form eschewed sculpture. The Romanesque style, of the eighth to twelfth centuries, was introduced to the United States in Richard Upjohn's Church of the Pilgrims (1844–1846) on Brooklyn Heights. The building originally had little external decoration, but in the mid 1960s acquired bronze relief plaques from the S.S. *Normandie*, made up into inappropriate portals (No. 34). The Romanesque Revival flourished, often with profuse ornamentation, during the last quarter of the nineteenth century, following construction of J. C. Cady's Museum of Natural History (1874–1877) at 77th Street and Central Park West. Several

of the carvings photographed are from this area of Manhattan, such as the leaf reliefs on West 85th and West 76th Streets from the 1890s (Nos. 58 & 143). The terracotta signature plate on the Brooklyn Heights hotel, the Margaret, also belongs to the period (No. 85). In 1929 a resurgence of Romanesque appeared, especially in the details of the Williamsburgh Savings Bank, Brooklyn (No. 74), and less so in those of the Hotel Lexington, Manhattan (No. 49). The character of these later Romanesque forms is similar to that of the stylized Near Eastern reliefs on the contemporaneous Knights of Pythias, Fred F. French and Transportation buildings.

Those two buildings that stimulated so much interest in brownstone, Trinity Church in Manhattan and the Church of the Holy Trinity in Brooklyn, are in the revival of the Gothic style, the successor to Romanesque and the culmination of medieval building. In New York, as one might expect, early brownstone row houses were in the Gothic manner. The boyhood home of Theodore Roosevelt, at 28 East 20th Street, and the more authentically preserved duplex on Brooklyn Heights, the Henry C. Bowen and George F. Thomas residences (1848) at 131 and 135 Hicks Street, retain hood molds over openings; the latter (the Roosevelt house was disfigured in renovation) has Tudor-arched entrances and tracery cast-iron railings to the front stairs.

Examples of sculpture within the time limits of the present collection belong to the eclectic and modern periods, and usually their details do not relate to the whole structure. An exception is in the persistence of the Gothic or "Christian" style, where consistency reigns throughout. An example is the canopy over a niche figure from the Church of Saint Mary the Virgin (1895) on West 46th Street (No. 109). Here are heads of a king, cardinal and martyrs serving as bosses at the bases of raking molds to gables capped by crockets. Other Gothic-manner adaptations of about the same time include figure supports on the Roosevelt Building (1893) at 841 Broadway (No. 15), the former Augustus Van Horn Stuyvesant house (1897) on East 79th Street (No. 30) and Tudor Gables, West 110th Street (Nos. 42 & 43). Belonging to the same category are sculptures on the later Woolworth Building (1913), for over a quarter of a century the world's tallest building, whose height was emphasized by the verticality of Gothic design (Nos. 18 & 19). Based upon a specific model but less integral with the building is a facsimile of the winged, horned simian "Penseur" of Notre Dame de Paris, made famous by Charles Méryon's etching half a century earlier, on a 1904 building off Fifth Avenue on East 39th Street (No. 41). Much of post-Civil War Gothic was inspired by Venetian, rather than north European, architecture, characterized by polychromy in stonework and stressed horizontals. The Montauk Club (1891) by Francis Kimball, adjoining Grand Army Plaza in Brooklyn, belongs to this phase. The lion, symbol of Saint Mark, patron saint of the Adriatic city, caps pedestal posts to the iron fence around the building (No. 16). Gothic décor continued through the 1920s, figuring on the School of Music and Art (1924; No. 88), the Murray Hill Building (1925; No. 65), Riverside Church (1927–1930; No. 98) Sherman Square Studios (1928; No. 87) and 81 Irving Place (1929; No. 8). The abrupt disappearance of Gothic at that time suggests that the Christian style may be counted among the casualties of the stock-market crash.

The rival style to Gothic Revival for brownstones in the mid-1800s was Renaissance Revival, inspired by palazzi and other edifices of the quattrocento. Early metropolitan examples are 38 West 12th Street (1842), Manhattan, and 13–15 Monroe Place (1850), Brooklyn Heights. The masterpiece is the Alexander M. White and Abiel Abbott Low duplex (1856–1857) on Pierrepont Place, also on the Heights. Italian Renaissance forms had been adopted slowly in western and northern Europe during the reigns of Louis XI and XII and Francis I in France (mid-fifteenth to mid-sixteenth century) and the Elizabethan and Jacobean periods (up to 1625) in England. The salamander, insignia of Francis I, figures on a brownstone (1892) on West 76th Street (No. 61) and in limestone (with fleur-de-lis patterns; 1906) on West 58th Street (No. 29). Also intermediary Gothic-Renaissance are the bird or griffin caryatid beasts of 1910 on East 62nd Street (No. 10) and the head emerging from foliage on West 55th Street (1882; No. 103).

A high Renaissance adaptation of the late seventies appears on the Long Island Historical Society Building on the Heights, with a full-round but engaged terracotta Viking's head in a spandrel (No. 124). The most handsome Renaissance complex in New York is the Henry Villard houses, designed in 1885 by McKim, Mead and White, built of brownstone on Madison Avenue opposite Saint Patrick's Cathedral. Four out of five residences, in three pavilions, face a courtyard. The architectural treatment is pure fifteenth-century Italian, and detailing both inside and out is or was exquisite, the reliefs outside having become badly eroded.

Spanish Renaissance design, sometimes referred to as provincial Italian, is called Plateresque after its resemblance to silversmith's work. This regional manner is reflected in the facade of the building at 302 West 86th Street (No. 66). North European Renaissance architecture often retained the steeply pitched medieval roof, which was masked by a parapet gable, to which classic motifs often related strangely, as on a Belgian-manner building on East 38th Street (No. 123).

The last flourish of the Renaissance idea in America was a movement known as Neo-Classic. It got off to a nationalistic start through the French gift of Frédéric-Auguste Bartholdi's Statue of Liberty, parts of which were exhibited at the Philadelphia Centennial of 1876, ten years before the entire allegorical figure was elevated on the pedestal by Richard Morris Hunt in New York harbor. Some of the best Neo-Classic sculptures in New York date from the turn of the century, no doubt a belated backwash from the impressiveness of the World's Columbian Exposition at Chicago (1892–1893), to which the East Coast architects R. M. Hunt and McKim, Mead and White contributed. The New York Supreme Court at Madison and 25th Street (No. 38), another building some thirty blocks uptown (No. 37) and the Dime Savings Bank of Brooklyn (1907; No. 137) display this near-peak of attainment. Surviving carvings from the destroyed Pennsylvania Station (1910) stand up well by comparison (No. 97), but similar work of a score of years later, on the Cable Building, is too "studied" (No. 51).

The quiet, intellectual, imitative original Renaissance style in Europe turned into the turbulent and emotional Baroque, which overran the Catholic world in the seventeenth century. A twentieth-century manifestation in New York is the doorway of The Darilton, west of Central Park (No. 126). The strenuous Baroque evolved into the playful and decadent Rococo, combining seashells, scrolls, streamers and symbols of amusement in vignette-like arrangements. Rococo influence shows in carvings over the portal of the old *Life* (humor magazine) building (No. 31) and on Amberg's Theatre (No. 82), both from the late nineteenth century.

Up to this point we have seen the evolution of between two and three thousand years of western culture related to a half century of New York architectural sculpture. The variety of metropolitan life nourished by such roots is in marked contrast to contemporary expression, in which period sources are hardly, if at all, discernible. Harbingers appeared in the 1890s. A rectangular panel, filled with floral forms and birds, anticipates a type of design that is practically geometric and was to be realized a quarter of a century later (No. 78). Reliefs in an upright panel on the New York and New Jersey Telephone Company Building (1898) on Willoughby Street, Brooklyn, make use of a contemporary telephone, with speaker and receiver, wire coils and bell or chimes (No. 72). By the *fin de siècle* the private townhouse was becoming a thing of the past, and carved or cast decorations henceforth would appear only on public and commercial buildings. The greater scale of such buildings and the elimination of traditional architectural dress dislodged sculpture from its accustomed roosts.

The first suggestion of the organic Art Nouveau (known also as Modern Style, Jugendstil, Sezession-stil and Stile Liberty) shows in the rhythmic lines of a mask with an abstract plant border on the panel of a knocker on the Montauk Club (No. 17). Art Nouveau is more fully developed in Louis Sullivan's Bayard Building (1898) on Bleecker Street (No. 112). Superficially Romanesque small round arches are coupled inside larger applied arches. Figures with outstretched arms are set on piers at their springing, providing a William Blake-like decorativeness that accentuates the richness of lesser motifs that Sullivan conceived with

fluency. A weird mask on the Combustion Engine Building (1925) on Madison Avenue is Art Nouveau in the manner of Aubrey Beardsley (No. 20).

Robert Kohn's Evening Post (later Garrison) Building has a traditional feeling, though all of its parts are original abstractions (No. 131). The fertility goddess—complete with cornucopia, pomegranates, grain, child with water blossoms, and tree of life supporting domestic animals—on the American Telephone & Telegraph Building (1917) is treated in a highly stylized manner, not unlike ancient Achaemenid work, resembling metalcraft (No. 84). A technique even more abstract, flat and linear, with incised outlines in the manner of the Egyptians, distinguishes an overdoor panel on the Ageloff Towers (1921) on East 3rd Street (No. 57). The antique Persian and Egyptian modes persisted for a score of years, the Persian reappearing in reliefs on the Fred F. French Building (1927; Nos. 107 & 108), 60 Wall Tower (1932; No. 128), the RCA Building (1933; No. 63) and the Federal Office Building (1935) at 90 Church Street (No. 155). The Egyptian may be traced through decorations on the Belmont Building (1924; No. 134), the Chanin Building (No. 113), the Horn & Hardart Automat on West 45th Street, Manhattan (No. 100) and the American Bank & Trust Company (1929), Brooklyn (No. 133) to the former Time and Life Building (1937), 1 Rockefeller Plaza (No. 110). The later examples show the full-blown style that marked the Paris Exposition des Arts Décoratifs of 1925.

The skyscraper presented few places for sculpture other than at the extremities of its harsh outlines; and on the Chrysler Building (1930), briefly the world's tallest until surpassed by the Empire State, are winged radiator caps as accents at the setbacks (No. 33). Embellishments such as these depended upon masonry, which persisted through the banded style up to World War II. Afterward it was replaced by the glass-slab high rise. Walls of glass reflect other identical walls, presenting a uniform shimmer that is devoid of relief on which the eye can rest. The total elimination of sculptured ornament had been accomplished.

Only a portion of the photographed sculptures have been referred to in this introduction, but these few are key examples which can serve as a guide

Introduction

to categorize the rest. Many changes occurred during the one hundred years covered. Early works were beholden to period styles and in some instances copied from specific monuments. During the eclectic phase no chronology can be established, as inspiration was a matter of individual choice. At the turn of the century a break with the past was effected, and new forms came into being. Soon afterward a new conception of architecture arose, which at first made little and then no provision for sculpture, which was added—if at all—as an extraneous makeshift. Today the sidewalk gallery of architectural sculpture is receding into the realm of historic curiosities. The awareness of a few individuals of the imminent destruction of this heritage led to the establishment of the Frieda Schiff Warburg Memorial Sculpture Garden at the Brooklyn Museum in the 1960s. Here "Fragmentary Landmarks," otherwise destroyed, find sanctuary for whatever edification and pleasure may be derived from dismembered mementoes of the city's past. Many subjects of the following plates soon will become candidates for such preservation. Hopefully many will be saved from the ignominy of burial as landfill.

CLAY LANCASTER

NOTE: The captions to the illustrations, in their fullest form, give the present and former names of the building; the address (all buildings are in Manhattan unless otherwise noted); then, in parentheses, the name of the architect or architectural firm and the date of the building (where the attribution is specifically to the sculptor, this is stated). Whenever part of this information is not given, it is either inapplicable or unobtainable.

1. 115 West 74th Street (1887).

2

3

4

2. Hudson Theatre, 139 West 44th Street
(J. B. McElfatsick & Sons, 1902).

3. 23 East 83rd Street.

4. 145 East 18th Street.

5. Birch Wathen School, originally Herbert N. Straus house, 9 East 71st Street (Horace Trumbauer, 1932).

6. 74 Trinity Place (remodeled 1925, 1934).

7. 312 West 73rd Street (Charles Pierrepont H. Gilbert, 1897).

8. 81 Irving Place (George Fred Pelham, 1929).

9. 15 East 77th Street (Robert Williams Gibson, 1898).

10. 40 East 62nd Street (A. J. Bodker, 1910).

8

9

10

11. Detail of "Asia," one of the four statuary groups outside the U.S. Customs House, Bowling Green (sculptor: Daniel Chester French, 1907).

12. New York Institute of Technology, formerly Temple of the Knights of Pythias, 135 West 70th Street (Thomas W. Lamb, 1926).

12

13

14

13. 55 Park Avenue (Fred F. French Co., 1922).

14. 55 Park Avenue.

15. Roosevelt Building, 841 Broadway (Stephen D. Hatch, 1893).

16

17

16. Montauk Club, Eighth Avenue and Lincoln Place, Brooklyn (Francis H. Kimball, 1891).

17. Montauk Club.

18

19

18. Woolworth Building, 233 Broadway (facade by John E. Donnelly, Jr., 1913; chief architect, Cass Gilbert).

19. Woolworth Building.

20. Combustion Engine Building, 200 Madison Avenue (Warren & Wetmore, 1925).

21. College of the City of New York, St. Nicholas Terrace between West 138th and 140th Streets (George B. Post, 1903–1907).

22. 262 West 77th Street (E. L. Angell, 1889).

23. 262 West 77th Street.

22

23

AVENUE
DU PARC
DE MONTSOURIS

24. 312 West 81st Street.

25. 1000 Park Avenue (Emery Roth, 1915).

26. "Br'er Rabbit and Tar-Baby," Brooklyn Public Library, Grand Army Plaza, Brooklyn (sculptor: Thomas Hudson Jones, 1941).

27. Eaves Building, 151 West 46th Street
(De Pace & Juster, 1928).

28. 59 West 76th Street (E. L. Angell, 1889).

29. Alwyn Court, 176 West 58th Street (Harde & Short, 1909).

30. Former Augustus Van Horn Stuyvesant house, 2 East 79th Street (N. H. Gilbert, 1897).

29

30

31. Hotel Clinton, formerly Life Building (the humor magazine *Life*), 19 West 31st Street (Carrère & Hastings, 1894).

32. Offices of The Museum of Modern Art,
originally George Blumenthal house, 23
West 53rd Street (Hunt & Hunt, 1902).

33. Chrysler Building, 405 Lexington Avenue (William Van Alen, 1930).

34. Bronze doors from *S.S. Normandie* (burned and sank in the Hudson River, 1942), Our Lady of Lebanon Roman Catholic Church, Remsen and Henry Streets, Brooklyn.

35. Gate, Bronx Zoo (sculptor: Paul Manship, 1934).

36. Monkey house, Central Park Zoo (sculptor: F. G. D. Roth, 1934).

37. 667 Madison Avenue (Horgan & Slattery, 1900).

36

37

38

38. New York Supreme Court, Appellate Division, Madison Avenue and 25th Street (architect: James Brown Lord, 1900; sculptor of seated figure "Force": Frederick Ruckstuhl).

39. Public School 116, 32nd Street between Second and Third Avenues (Thomas J. Waters Co., Builders, 1925).

40

40. Head of the artist J. A. M. Whistler, 4 East 39th Street (George B. Post & Sons, 1904).

41. 4 East 39th Street.

42. Tudor Gables, 527 West 110th Street (Waid & Willauer, 1909).

43. Tudor Gables.

41

42

43

44

45

44. Bank of Tokyo, formerly American Surety Company, 100 Broadway (Bruce Price, 1895).

45. Blue Ribbon Inn, 145 West 44th Street.

46. Former Vanderbilt Hotel, 4 Park Avenue (Warren & Wetmore, 1912).

47

48

47. John and Gold Streets (Springsteen &
Goldhammer, 1930).

48. New York City Civil Court, 111 Centre
Street (sculptor: William Zorach, 1960).

49. Hotel Lexington, 511 Lexington Avenue
(Schultze & Weaver, 1929).

50. Federal Reserve Bank of New York, 33 Liberty Street (York & Sawyer, 1924).

51. Cable Building, 611 Broadway (before 1931).

52

53

54

52. 920 Broadway (Schwartz & Gross, 1916).

53. R. H. Macy & Co., 34th Street between Broadway and Seventh Avenue (De-Lemos & Cordes, 1901).

54. 24 East 95th Street (Thomas Graham, c. 1899).

55

56

55. London Terrace garden, 425 West 23rd Street (Farrar & Watmaugh, 1930).

56. Manufacturer's Hanover Trust Company, formerly Brooklyn Trust Company, 177 Montague Street, Brooklyn (York & Sawyer, 1915).

57. Ageloff Towers, 141 East 3rd Street (Shampon & Shampon, 1929).

58

58. 333 West 85th Street (Ralph S. Townsend, 1890).

59. Heads of Franklin Delano Roosevelt and Sigmund Freud, 11 West 73rd Street (building 1902, decorations later).

60. Parkchester, 1936 East Tremont Avenue, Bronx (Richmond H. Shreve et al., 1938–1942).

61

61. 161 West 76th Street (1892).

62. Parkchester, 1946 East Tremont Avenue, Bronx (see No. 60).

63. 49th Street entrance, RCA Building, 30 Rockefeller Plaza (sculptor: Leo Friedlander, 1933).

62

63

64

65

64. Puck Building, 295–309 Lafayette Stree[
(Albert Wagner, 1885, 1892).

65. Murray Hill Building, 285 Madison Ave
nue (Rouse & Goldstone, 1925).

66. 302 West 86th Street (Joseph H. Taft
1888).

67. Dakota Apartments, 1 West 72nd Street (Henry J. Hardenbergh, 1884).

68. 3 Riverside Drive (Charles Pierrepont H. Gilbert, 1896).

69. ITT Building, 67 Broad Street (Buchman & Kahn, 1926).

70. Webster Hall, 119–125 East 11th Street (Charles Rentz, 1886).

71. 16 Park Avenue (Fred F. French Co., 1924).

72

73

72. Former New York and New Jersey Tele
phone Company Building, 81 Willough
by Street, Brooklyn (Andrew C. McKen
zie, 1898).

73. Associated Press Building, 50 Rockefelle
Plaza (sculptor: Isamu Noguchi, 1940).

74. Williamsburgh Savings Bank, 1 Hanso
Place, Brooklyn (Halsey, McCormick &
Helmer, 1929).

74

75. 110 West 40th Street (Buchman & Fox, 1912).

76. Element from a demolished building, sculpture garden of the Brooklyn Museum, Eastern Parkway and Washington Avenue, Brooklyn.

77. 313 West 74th Street (Charles Pierrepont H. Gilbert, 1893).

78. 14 West 71st Street (G. A. Schellenger, 1891).

79. 340 West 84th Street (1888).

78

79

80. Birch Wathen School (see No. 5).

81. 144 West 55th Street (William B. Baldwin, 1881; the decoration is later).

82

83

82. Former Amberg's Theatre and Irving Place Theatre, Irving Place between 14th and 15th Streets (1888).

83. Bronx County Building, 851 Grand Concourse, Bronx (sculptor: Adoph A. Weinman, 1933).

84. American Telephone & Telegraph Building, 195 Broadway (Welles Bosworth, 1917).

85. Hotel Margaret, 1 Orange Street, Brooklyn (Frank Freeman, 1889).

86. Palazzo d'Italia, 620 Fifth Avenue (sculptor: Giacomo Manzù, 1965).

88

87. Sherman Square Studios, 160 West 73rd Street (Tillion & Tillion, 1928).

88. Fiorello H. LaGuardia School of Music and Art—originally Teachers Training School—135th Street between Convent Avenue and St. Nicholas Terrace (William H. Gompert, 1924).

89. Brooklyn Academy of Music, 30 Lafayette Avenue, Brooklyn (Herts & Tallant, 1908).

90. Hotel Aberdeen, 17 West 32nd Street (H. B. Mulliken, 1902).

91. 380 Riverside Drive (1906).

92. College of the City of New York (see No. 21).

89

90

91

92

93

94

93. Horn & Hardart Automat, 155 West 33rd Street (Louis Allan Abramson, 1930).

94. 56 Morton Street (Josiah Lindsey, 1891).

95. Radio City Music Hall, 50th Street and Avenue of the Americas (sculptor: Hildreth Meière, c. 1940).

96

97

96. Mark Hellinger Theatre, formerly Holly-
wood Theatre, 237 West 51st Street
(1929).

97. Element from the demolished Pennsyl-
vania Station, sculpture garden of the
Brooklyn Museum (station by McKim,
Mead & White, 1910).

98. Riverside Church, Riverside Drive and
West 122nd Street (Charles Collens &
Henry C. Pelton, 1927–1930).

99. Former Crowell-Collier Building, 640 Fifth Avenue (1949–1950).

00. Horn & Hardart Automat, 103 West 45th Street (F. P. Platt & Bros., 1929).

01. 218 East 27th Street (Charles Rentz, 1890).

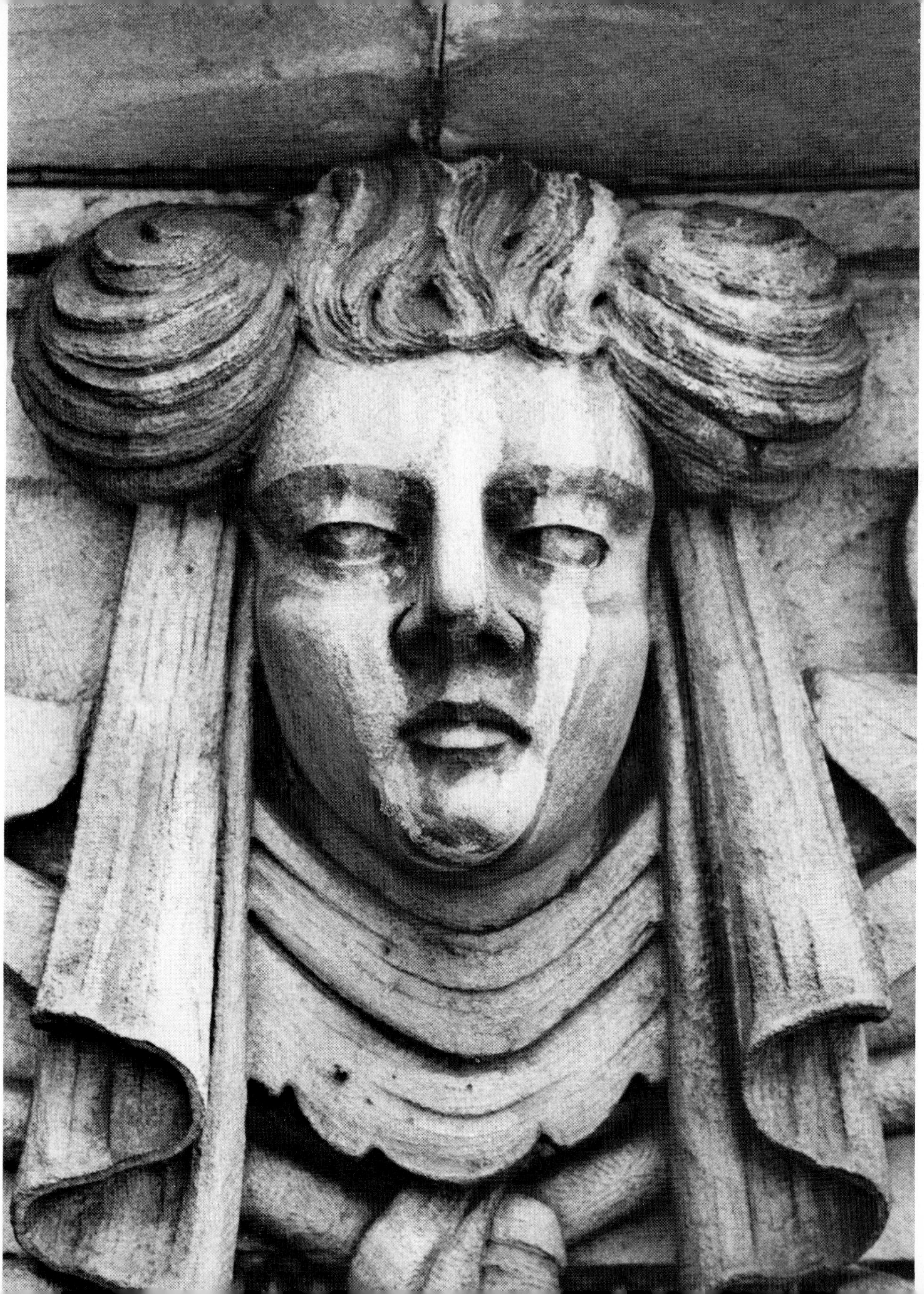

102. Colosseum, 435 Riverside Drive (Schwartz & Cross, 1910).

103. 200 West 55th Street (1882).

104. Elephant Building, 44–53 Westchester Square, Bronx (Maximilian Zipkes, 1925).

105. Transportation Building, 225 Broadway (1928).

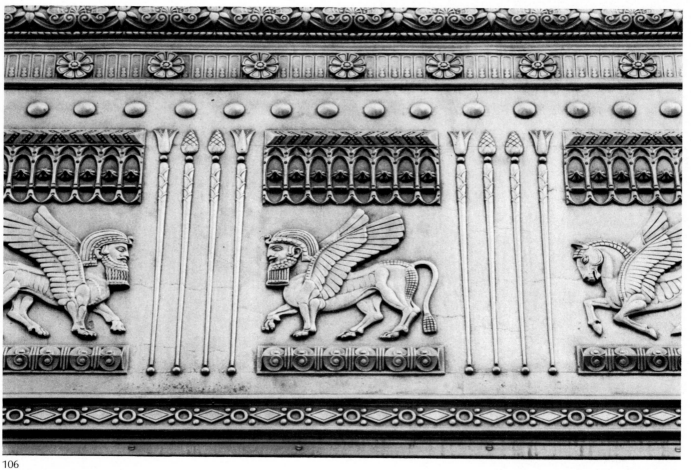

106

106. Fred F. French Building, 551 Fifth Avenue (Fred F. French Co., 1927).

107. Fred F. French Building.

108. Fred F. French Building.

107

108

109. Church of St. Mary the Virgin, 145 West 46th Street (Napoleon Le Brun, 1895).

110. The 14 West 49th Street entrance of the General Dynamics Building, formerly Time and Life Building, 1 Rockefeller Plaza (sculptor: Lee Lawrie, 1937).

111. General Dynamics Building: the 15 West 48th Street entrance (sculptor: Attilio Piccirilli, 1937).

110

111

112. Bayard Building, formerly Condict Building, 65 Bleecker Street (Louis Sullivan, 1898).

113. Chanin Building, 122 East 42nd Street (Sloan & Robertson, 1929).

114

115

114. 720 Park Avenue (Rosamo Caudela, 1928).

115. 136 Waverly Place.

116. New York Life Insurance Building, 51 Madison Avenue (Cass Gilbert, 1928).

117

117. New York Stock Exchange, 8 Broad Street (George B. Post; pediment sculptors: John Quincy Adams Ward and Paul Bartlett, 1903).

118. Hart Building, 100 West 42nd Street (Sidney Daub, 1924).

118

119

120

119. 317 West 103rd Street (1890s).

120. 20 West 75th Street (John C. Burne, 1889).

121. 314 West 71st Street (1893).

122. 146th Street and Broadway (1912).

123. 149 East 38th Street (Ralph S. Townsend, 1902).

124

124. Long Island Historical Society, 128 Pierrepont Street, Brooklyn (George B. Post, 1878).

125. Fuller Building, 45 East 57th Street (Walker & Gillette, 1928).

126

127

126. The Dorilton, 171 West 71st Street (Janes & Leo, 1900).

127. The Dorilton.

128. 60 Wall Tower, 70 Pine Street, (Clinton & Russell, 1932).

129. 60 Wall Tower.

128

129

130. New York Academy of Medicine, 2 East
103rd Street (York & Sawyer, 1926).

131. Garrison Building, formerly New York Evening Post Building, 20 Vesey Street (Robert D. Kohn, 1906).

132

133

132. 119 West 40th Street (Robert Julius Maynicke & Franke, 1912).

133. American Bank & Trust Co., 185 Montague Street, Brooklyn (Corbetot, Harrison & MacMurray, 1929).

134. Belmont Building, 181 Madison Avenue (1924).

135

136

135. Hearst Magazine Building, 969 Eighth Avenue (1926).

136. 25th Hook & Ladder Company, 205 West 77th Street (Horgan & Slattery, 1900).

137. The Dime Savings Bank of Brooklyn, 9 DeKalb Avenue at Albee Square, Brooklyn (Halsey, McCormick & Helmer, 1907).

THE DIME SAVINGS BANK OF BROOKLYN

137

138

138. Maritime Exchange Building, 80 Broad Street (Sloan & Robertson, 1930).

139. 107 West 69th Street (1886).

140. 42 Morton Street (M. C. Merritt, 1889).

141. 134 West 69th Street.

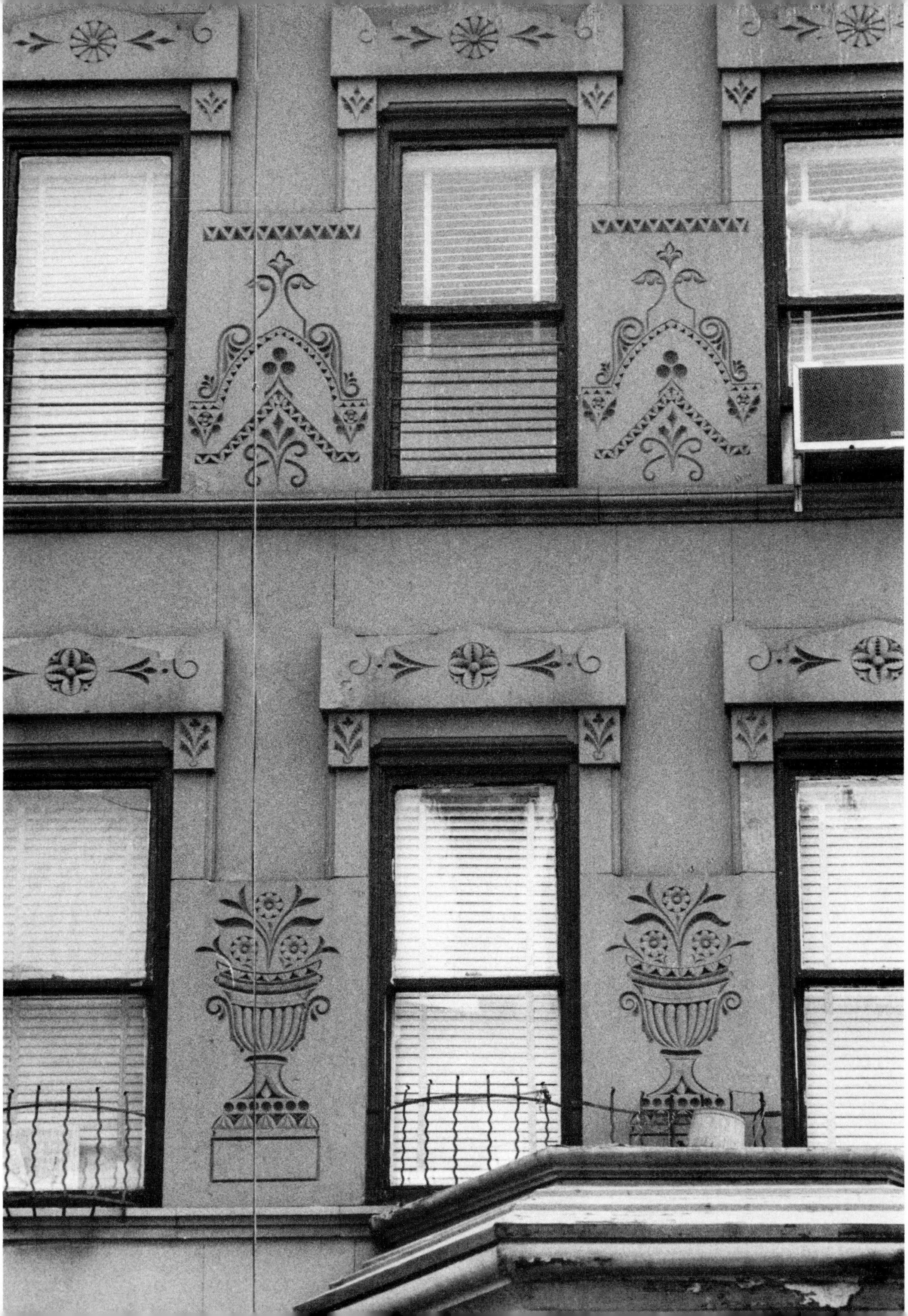

142

142. 55–59 Beaver Street (James Brown Lord, 1894).

143. 53 West 76th Street (1899).

144

145

147

144. First National City Trust Co., originally City Bank Farmers Trust Co., 24 Exchange Place / 22 William Street (Cross & Cross, 1931; the buffalo nickel was designed by James Earle Fraser).

145. Italian Consulate General, originally Henry P. Davidson house, 690 Park Avenue (Walker & Gillette, 1917).

146. 43–47 West 23rd Street (Henry J. Hardenbergh, 1894).

147. 124 East 40th Street (Laurence F. Peck, 1922).

146

148. "Ethel Barrymore," I. Miller Shoe Building, 1552 Seventh Avenue (sculptor: Alexander Stirling Calder; building, 1916; statues, 1929).

149. 315 West 103rd Street (M. V. B. Ferndon, 1891; remodeled).

150. 95 Madison Avenue (Barney & Colt, 1911).

151. 120 Riverside Drive (George Keister, 1899).

152. Wall and Hanover Building, 59 Wall Street (Delano & Aldrich, 1927).

153. 226 West 4th Street (Fred J. Miller, 1890).

154. 157–159 West 74th Street (1886).

155. Federal Office Building, 90 Church Street (Cross & Cross, 1935).

154

155

156

158

157

156. The Institute of Aeronautical Sciences, originally Edward Berwind house, 2 East 64th Street (N. C. Mellon, 1896).

157. 1080 Park Avenue (Mott B. Schmidt, 1925).

158. 135 Cedar Street.

159. 56–58 Pine Street (Oswald Wirz, 1893).

159